Invisible Mink

Invisible Mink

Poems

Jessie Janeshek

Iris Press
Oak Ridge, Tennessee

Copyright © 2010 by Jessie Janeshek

All rights reserved. No portion of this book may be reproduced in any form or by any means, including electronic storage and retrieval systems, without explicit, prior written permission of the publisher, except for brief passages excerpted for review and critical purposes.

Cover Painting, "Four Women"
Copyright © 2010 by Cynthia Markert

Iris Press is an imprint of the Iris Publishing Group, Inc.
www.irisbooks.com

Design: Robert B. Cumming, Jr.

Library of Congress Cataloging-in-Publication Data

Janeshek, Jessie, 1980-
Invisible mink : poems / Jessie Janeshek.
   p. cm.
ISBN 978-1-60454-211-0 (pbk. : alk. paper)
I. Title.
PS3610.A5683I68 2010
811'.6—dc22
                                              2010035533

Acknowledgments

The following publications first printed these poems from *Invisible Mink*: *Blue &Yellow Dog:* "Holiday, Cuba," "Jezebel 5(6)," and "Love in a Fireproof Box (or Jezebel speaks to her Eva Phillips self)." *Otoliths:* "Flaming June" and "Sorry, Wrong Number." *Rougarou:* "This is the 20th Century, and We Get to New York on Time." *Moria:* "Love Means Never Having to Say You're Sorry."

Marilyn Kallet, my friend and mentor, has provided me with innumerable opportunities to expand the meaning and scope of my poetry and to share my work with others at the University of Tennessee–Knoxville and beyond. I began drafting several of these poems during a workshop she taught for the Virginia Center for the Creative Arts in Auvillar, France. As she read (and reread) this manuscript, she offered me comments and suggestions that have made *Invisible Mink* a much stronger book than it would have been otherwise. Her wisdom, empathy, and generosity are unmatched. Arthur Smith, Ben Lee, and Chris Holmlund patiently read and remarked on this manuscript with humor, intelligence, and encouragement. Earlier in my career, Larry E. Grimes, Elizabeth M. Hull, Peter Jay Shippy, and Bill Knott radically influenced my growth as a writer of poetry, sometimes with growing pains, but always with the good of my work in mind. I am lucky to know all of them.

The University of Tennessee–Knoxville provided a subvention from the Hodges' Fund to help finance the publication of *Invisible Mink*. Thank you to Charles Maland for making that subvention possible.

Cynthia Markert kindly offered her painting, "Four Women," for the cover of the book.

Casa Libre en la Solana in Tucson, AZ, was another place where several of these poems began. Thank you to Ann Fine and Kristen Nelson for allowing me to complete two artist residencies at Casa. I put the final touches on the manuscript during my residency at Helen Chellin's Red Cinder Creativity Center on the Big Island of Hawaii, and I am thankful she has created such a haven for writers and artists.

I am grateful to Drew Johnson; my parents Joe Janeshek and Claudia Janeshek; Man Ray, Villette, and Callie; my friends Pam Rowland and Amber Partin; and my grandparents, Paul Harris (1925-2009) and Pearl Harris. My grandfather made me want to be a writer, and I believe he would be proud to see this book.

Preface

Jessie Janeshek's poetry does much more than flirt with vintage films. The poems take in the films like rescued kittens, pamper them, let them play and grow strong. While a lot of contemporary poetry seems grim and lacks a sense of playfulness, Jessie Janeshek's work never loses its wit, love of adventure, and of risk.

"It's staying light later," the narrator of the opening poem tells us, "I'm in the mood to meditate Bette Davis...." The poems deliver verses on seductive female stars from the films of the 1930s and beyond. Like the stars they're watching, the poems become the empowered ones; language is theirs to play with, to betray ("How did the wedding ring slip off Pat's finger?")

Each poem is impeccably crafted, syllable by syllable. The line breaks are as crisp as a good Pinot Grigio. No, wait, for the Bette and Lucy poems, pour yourself a martini. The Perpignan poems might like a tumbler of rosé.

Jaunty, adventuresome, these poems take matters into their own hands and toy with them. Jezebel may have a bad rep, but remember, in poetry as in movie-watching, no one gets hurt. The art of art is the play and the catharsis. We readers or viewers get to walk away unscathed. Not one single dyed hair will be harmed!

Jessie's poems have "Bette Davis Eyes." You know the pop song. But what does that mean? Means that you can look into them for a long time, fall for them, fall deep, and that they will never love you back—not unless you think poems have a life of their own—as some of us poets do believe.

These lyrical, rhythmically lively pieces do much to remind us of the way powerful women in film and in poetry can inspire us humans to interact more gracefully. Enjoy all the connections and the word play that frees the imagination. Perhaps they were "inspired by leisure," as well as by struggle. It's your leisure now, hard-won, to be sure. The poems stand on their own, without props. Put the ring back on. In sickness, in health, Jessie's work will never let you down.

—Marilyn Kallet

Marilyn Kallet is the author of 14 books, including Packing Light: New and Collected Poems *(Black Widow Press.) She directs the creative writing program at the University of Tennessee.*

Contents

1.

The Appledoppeling Gang • 15
Jezebel, Jealous of Television • 16
"This Is the 20th Century, and We Get to New York on Time" • 17
Restless Palms • 19
Derry Queen. Venus in Furs. • 20
Love Means Never Having to Say You're Sorry • 21
Tale of Three Cities • 24
Vivisect the Creamy Sister • 26
Jezebel Keeps the Appointment • 27

2.

Beyond Self-Help • 31
Life's Work • 32
Lucy in Wien, Looking at Brueghel's *Hunters in Snow* • 33
Jezebel, Void of Course • 34
Post-*Villette*, Part Deux • 36
Prayer for Lucy, December 23rd • 37
Lucy Snowe, Ordinary Day • 38
Lucy to Erzebet, Watching *Conquest* • 39
Eagle, Moose, Grizzly   Revisited • 40
Classic • 41
Merrily • 42
Thrift • 43

3.

Island Girl • 47
Working Girl, Perpignan • 49
J & J Radio: Island Girl Dialogue • 50
Working Girl 2 • 52
Island Girl 2 • 53

Belle-Souer • 54
Holiday, Cuba • 55
Flaming June • 58
Sorry, Wrong Number • 61
Jezebel Interludes • 64
Jezebel 5(6) • 65
Love in a Fireproof Box
    (or Jezebel speaks to her Eva Phillips self) • 67
Jezebel, Out of the Nursery • 68

4.

Preamble • 71
"Mares eat oats and does eat oats"
    Charles and Mary Lamb eat Shakespeare… • 73
Mock Ghazaling in the Nursery • 74
When and If Jezebel Waxes Brunette • 75
Lucy Snowe Thinks *Dark Victory,* Cannot Commit Herself • 77
Jezebel Has the Same Mole as Alexis. Hers Is Not Velvet. • 78
Why Jezebel Writes Saturday (She Could Be Sleeping) • 79
Jezebel Intermezzos • 80
Poseidon Adventure, Plus One • 81
Poseidon Adventure, Plus Two • 83
For Mary, Miscarriage • 84
Poseidon Adventure, Plus Three • 85
Theme Song (a straight, light, and peppy poem) • 86
Letter to Mary from Jezebel • 87
Poseidon Adventure, Plus Four • 88
Another Morning After • 89

Notes • 91

I.

The Appledoppeling Gang

It's staying light later. I'm in the mood
to meditate Bette Davis, bookend the world
with her *Stolen Life* twins. How can one work in

Pat and Kate Bosworth, the concept of want
the idea of root canals, the dream where my neighbor
wears a Great Dane's head like a fucked-up Magritte?

Pat and Kate Bosworth want the same man.
The waves rocking that Massachusetts light house
uproot Mother Nature, beat her to a pulp.

Thirty days make a habit, and being an artist
isn't so rare. Pat wears fur to a square dance
courts Bill in her long evening skirt. Kate's portraits

are neat, Whistlerish. Her west-side gallery
serves caviar. Karnock's a pig, but at least
he takes risks. He'll paint either sister, dead or alive.

How did the wedding ring slip off Pat's finger?
Kate wanted harder, pushed past Pat's right-to-
left lunar. The dog-eat-dog neighbor pulsed smoke
through her mask. Not enough moon? Add some gloss.

Jezebel, Jealous of Television

She says she's my necessary fiction
thinks I watch too much
need to shift off the grey beach
haphazardly-parked '41 Lincoln
happy platinum woman
spinning with ice cream.

Spring's coming in with her fever
vomito. Clock's lost an hour
hot molasses tastes like cotton.
Jane made body races
in the wheelchair routine
two nights pre-beach.

This movie's what we inhabit.
Sisters know too much about one another
but at least no one's Gloria Swanson.
Though I miss Victor Buono
I'm pushing through
fresh coat of lipstick, Victory Red

method acting. Even when angry
Jezebel'll praise me. Grey's the only word
I spell pretentiously. No colour
no flavour, I'm not big on labour.
This poem will never
be a sestina. Leisure's

my inspiration, Blanche
tied to her pulley
teeth popping out when she dies.
Jane's babied by lamplight
quietly scanning
her scrapbooks and I understand.

"This Is the 20th Century, and We Get to New York on Time"

Yesterday I met
the medicine man
his sunshine fruit tablets
lit my hope like a fireball
train windows stained glass
by his vitamin light.
He said my aura was green.

I hate east. At least riding west
the new year comes over and over.
John says we're actors.
This Is All There Is.
        The chinchilla coat, Sadie
    yes, with real lace!

Day 8, baked Alaska for supper.
Would I a baby
had I stayed Mildred Plotka?
Would I a rascally nipple?
Would I throw her to Dickens
let her be raised
by a jeweled foster grandma
cut angels from silk?

Last night almost ate
a full box of cookies
tossed the rest out the window, Indianapolis.
Should have saved them for gypsies
not hoboes.
        I was human once
I read Lawrence.
"Pale love lost in a snow of fear"
I cheat now, getting paid
to read scripts. It's cannibalistic

telling the men their novels are lovely
though he did write I was shapely
with Saturn eyes.
                      "My little
white Madonna," John says
"don't try to put it inside."
                      Nothing important.
          The garland's in my name.
Though I ask how much steam
one can burn mourning.

Restless Palms

Why this slow crawl
through February?
I listen to the flick
of my cat's feather-light ears
can't bear to think

this might be my stride.
Imbalance and balance?
Synonymous. The scale lady's
arm muscles bulge
above one glowing blue eye.

I bought twenty headbands
at the underground Montreal drugstore
never wore one. Three Lucies canoodle
corner booth of my mind.
Histrionically shaky

after two cups of coffee
I live off sweetness and blight
rise every day
to skate on Veronica Lake.
She's frankly lit

by a border of torches
shaped like a small constellation.
Hotdogs roast on her rotating blades
smell astrological.
You get used to her moods.

Derry Queen. Venus in Furs.

Age comes fast in Aberdeen.
Age comes fast for men wanted.

Dixie cup of ice cream on the shores
of the Don and the Dee, whiter city than Brighton.

Pollutia reminds me of Weirton
so hard when everything's touching.

Roman tour guide, Vienna
curly-haired waiter named Joe.

Half-caf espresso, kiss from Brazil
an ice rink is just too damn honest.

Crystal's rolling on uppers again
seeing her father (he died, she was small).

Chopped cod, a restaurant
ping-pong genies in theatres

or what do foreign cities mean in dreams?

Smells like home, ocean
I wade through trash, feeling safe.

Paul never made it to Russia. Defrost. Gnosticate.
Don't write back either.

Love Means Never Having to Say You're Sorry

I bled from my breasts for a month
attended my wake incognito
on the arm of a Cincinnati mob-boss.

How **blonde** Tony's date is!
    Would she like a slice of stewed melon?

Cradling the jackpot chunk
envisioning my body
spread on checkered cloth

instead of green olives
I spat seeds in the small well
of my cream Chinette plate

let the pink meat
decompose in my throat
sat at the piano sure they'd bust me.

No other woman plays *Clair de Lune*
like the Charleston.
Rossini for Tony
Linus and Lucy
a little out of tune…

Some dimwit dug out
    the pimientos!

Chanel heels sunk in mud.
I shrunk while I smooched him goodbye.

He disappeared with his chauffer.
I went to the river, whipping my wig off.

My lungs cleared in July
month made for uprooting lovers
crabs, rubies, and gold
waxing crescent, last of midnight

black kidskin shoes
in a T-shape.

Lay snails on a dish.
Will they trace his initials
in raspberry gunk?

Month of laburnium…wait!
They write *Québec City*.

My Montreal cabbie
wears a bone through his nose.
His seats smell like Allspice and newsink.
Purple dusk ruts for light

goes to bed hungry.
Eat a jar of Nutella.
Skip the obituaries.

Sun's melting crystal.
I walk past a chapel
looking for birds
even brown rabbits
Mary's face smoothed
with cold Oil of Olay.
God the cold!

Did she shake her head no?

My hand's turning blue.
I'd have come sooner
had I the money. Yes I'd have stood
the mosquitoes, I love you!

Old woman walks past
dragging her market cart
canned milk, frozen lemons
gasps at the day moon
moan of the clock bells
asks   *déjà midi?*

Tale of Three Cities

1. You spend underground days
shuffling through tunnels
desperate for jars of Nutella.
Chocolately gloss
chases backache pills down.

You surface nightly
walk Vieux Montreal   eating kebabs
shove your nose in the needles
of blue-lighted pine trees.

Men in tobaggans   pocked by snowgrit
kick you from payphones
make you move South.

2. Lists, things to do
saber-toothed cats
the hope to get through—
life-cycling Bogart
and Bacall movie marathons
barely dulls pain.

        Climb the hanging stairs   of your Frisco condo
        in sequined palazzos.

        Serve your lover vodka
        from the geometric bar.

        Face wrapped in bandages
        he smokes through a holder

        glass straw leading
        to his beet juice-stained mouthole.

Would you like a smoke now?

When he smooches adieu
leaves sans a trenchcoat
you'll blast the phonograph

        Goddamit if he doesn't get arrested!

stand guard at the TV
make sure they tape
your only light passage
a call from the dealers
checking on the car you don't drive.

Vivisect the Creamy Sister

The dragon painter lost his process
      once he found his princess   she drowned but resurrected
  post-exhibit

New poems sit colon-heavy on my chest
    soft apostrophes are burdens with the bullets in their heads

        White time's interstitial, solid light through each second
        Black time is lifelike, sleep orthodox

Ovules spinning from the voxbox one option
        expansive—scratch—exclusive love

Redeem your seventh winter as the bride
    focus on the lightning that could have stretched behind your ears

thoughts beneath your skull   a crossbone-wide

Jezebel Keeps the Appointment

Write it out *hard*, you scream.
Watching *Midnight Express*
let me dream I busted in a kid's skull
left enough blood for an oath.

The rest of the boys do light math
remind me you have a bad heart
someday you'll slip off, comatose
leave me to calculate grace and want.

Last night, the cat pissed the bed.
I washed so many times
couldn't get clean
dictated a letter to Lady Macbeth.

You're not the weak one
your braids sopapillas.
You're not the cute little ruin.

The train does not stop here.
What's worse? It's packed
with people from high school.

I don't think they know me
hepped up, not desperate.
I won't earnestly pray
or die for just anything.

You want to give, don't know
how to give up. I want to keep writing
*There's no guarantee. There's
no guarantee.* This comforts me.

2.

Beyond Self-Help

The hand that rocks the cradle
rocks the concubine.
Two Lucies kneel under pine
arms stretched in the posture of want.
One must have dark to watch
Ninotchka, sketch her ecriture
nocturne on grey serge. Another needs
barren trees, snowfall sans teeth.
One loves bouncing fire. One doubts
her cardinal will last until Friday.
Both hate the fill, could come
to love filling, come in
where their starsister sits
vicereine sipping her vichyssoise.

Life's Work

Thirty-six days since Christmas
doubting these dregs
ever did nourish
December a sardine
sexless and dark.

Six vast yellow eyes
hiss in the window
eagle, moose, grizzly
your skin so pink.

"Lucy Snowe, an *oie blanche*?"
"Pa," I sniff, "Hardly."
Posed in prose
fine minx of a Janus
she doesn't mind hard work
never forgets.
          What news from France?
Ginevra in a marathon
with *la bonne gentilhomme*?
Coleridge's Geraldine
harmless as shadow?

Dear Lucy, you light
my paragraph fire, stitch cheer
toward an end, and where
can that leave me? Out back
hacking up words.

Lucy in Wien, Looking at Brueghel's *Hunters in Snow*

Dogs taunt the hunt
with their curlicued tails.
Peer toward the haze. Is that the tip
of a Romantic background castle?

Fated match of crack-the-whip
a child drops to the seafoam-chrome ice
stares up, concussed
to the seafoam-chrome sky.

Where would I be in this painting?
Slippery woman, mossy hair
sliding under my cap?
Baby sealed in a wine barrel
instead of a cradle?

High on the battlements
awaiting a sweet virgin singer?
She'll choke on my
deep-chocolate teacake
treble clef scratching her throat.

Jezebel, Void of Course

Four days beyond Twelfth Night
    world blanched as hay
our moon rose the fattest
    she will all season   so cloudy
Jezebel missed it   now months
will butt sideways   crescent
of wifelight.

Jezebel's posture is bad.   No thick books
    to put on her head   wants to read voraciously
crunch pages like chips
      crush a stick to her back?

Is it true in cold weather
      she resorts to writing on friendship?
         that true friendship strangles?   bitter spiced wreath?

Last night, ignored Hugo   who jumped in the leopard-skinned
      shower behind her.

Breed, breed a peach.   Jezebel bellied.
      Who owns "chianti"?   Feels like a flake.

Poetry ages. She's reusing cheese three years old.

The moon moves away as you read this
    soon 50 days to wreathe earth.

Jezebel never paints nails
        prays at the threshold of sex

still shakes the polish
once in a while, though.

Post-*Villette*, Part Deux

Lucy cleans the stained glass with the whoreheart of a rabbit
Lucy slaps the bald ass of the bleached-blonde Swedish saint
Lucy spritzes holier-than-thou parfum
through his boudoir   Lucy's pupils macaroon

Lucy grooms her feathers with untarnished tines of ice
Lucy files her fingerclaws on Monsieur Fontanbleu
Lucy plates her accidental fugue
uncoiling like a snailshell sous la lune

Prayer for Lucy, December 23rd

So what if today's not the day
to re-enact *Diabolique* in my brain?
I still eat plantains, contemplate moss doilies
yammer on top of the hologrammed pool

light a candle for you, sweet Miss Lucy,
treat it the February way. Little grimalkin
I bless, let your grey down
merry myrrh girl I sing

"murder is brisk, our souls chilly."
What I love about winter?
No yule, just lily. Candied
suites deck the memory glands.

Lucy Snowe, Ordinary Day

She takes to drinking loosely in the afternoon, noix de cocoa soda blessed with scotch. Rotten lemon hanging off the glass like cocktail shrimp, she saunters up the hill to palm the slot machine, inhales violent coffee topped with chocolate by the spoonful, somersaults back down to learn her French, watches *Naughty Marietta* via satellite instead, knocks outside to hang the laundry, asks the rooster to her chambre for two rounds of roulette. Russian with the pampered goats from Roussillon.

Lucy to Erzebet, Watching *Conquest*

Horses storm the parlor, latest in Russian décor.
I know I promised to take this poem easy
make her last, half past four. I spent February
on chicken boullion, writing around you
and Brueghel. *Ice green chrome sky.*
Do liquid diets strain your lyric voice pure?
Everything was a spectacle, or nothing was.

The train tracks my head, breaks at my right ear.
The *do not disturb*? Yes, dear, it's for you.
Mary's garden of eggs dangles off trees.
Puffy EBs fluff the monogrammed bedsheets.
Garbo overpins her brows to the stage
Cossacks invading her décolletage. Charles
Boyer's shoulders arch under his bullions.
I'm petrified, per usual, to let my mind trot

even though you quote Hopkins, *"thursh's
eggs look little low heavens and thrush,"*
ask *what's the rush, chicki-poo?*
Gabrielle paints a new desert each day in pastels
can't read French, calls them lilypad Waterloos
anyway. I need more Villon, but fuck guilt
so much Ivory soap snowing in the proscenium.

Eagle, Moose, Grizzly   Revisited

No longer out back
  in bed with the aixes
counting out days
the black beetle tinkeled
I need to watch
spy Jezebel out of my love
happy Peter Lorre
knew how to burn
Crystal wasn't so lucky
  babified
make it stick"
it becomes an addiction
don't reheat my tea
Europe's a crutch
of this ruckus.

hacking up words

salad so fresh
  where has the night gone?
    Jekyll and Hyde
    triangle of eye
reared himself a gentleman
  the Corncracker ticket.
    but Icy was warm
    " a girl who could lie
    I do anything twice
      I mean it
    too thirsty to write
      please lift me out

Classic

Time to write a poem
like a Warner Bros. film
fast-flash, all process
limbs of the body in check.
Don't come to the poetry chair
trussed up like Tom Powers
on his last visit home.
Reporters pick stories
out of silk pockets
chisel them into horsepills
your crowd washes down
with black gin. Speak easy
thank talkies, thank Jack
you're not stuck in the bowery
chestnut shells twisted
by immigrant children.
Who says your Bogey
poems aren't erotic
the knock-outs, the unholy three
Cagney, Eddie G.
already parodying characters
2 years into the genre.
Make it to the top
you get modern architecture
a chrome bar you can hide
under the phonograph, a star
in your gut from the gat.
Joan Blondell slammed down toast
ran to the bathroom
came back to another movie
3 days per month off for cramps.

Merrily

Everyone smoking.   Handwritten notes.   The need for a priest
  penetrates the ruined chapel

Diana Boyce-Smith baking buns on the side
                      scorching her throat with tea, rationed sugar

sandwiched between   the blue-suited American
    and the chap who'll go blind.

Daddy's old-fashioned windows illuminate study
    beautiful soup!
                Please don't tell Diana

art-deco collars are anachronistic in 1916

    don't exchange engagement rings
with both brother and mate.   Hyperventilate

conversations with "quite."   Turn the clock to the wall
and you'll have to come thrice.   It'll be dark
    roses dying.   Boys leave for the front

in five hours.   Cross not a finger.   Cross not a prayerbook
Switch airplanes and boats.   Rich. Neutral. Removed.

Don't all little girls   crush on their fathers
        ride the violence of envy the way a man can't?

Thrift

Velveteen reader, do you have a fever?
Your velveteen writer does. Button-eyed saint
called the plumber two lines too late
but Niagara won't fall. In *Remember the Night*
Barbara Stanwyck's not lethal. MacMurray
will save her from jail. Plumber's clogged up
with cancer, his St. Terese candle cost 99 cents.
Babs pinched her bracelet off the velveteen plate
not lethal, just hurting, loves Fred MacMurray
like a clogged-up tornado. Cancer's not
always early, plumbers sometimes pop buttons.
Niagara Falls glitters when lines disappoint.

3.

Island Girl

Personal disintegration, no underwear, heat.
Played Old Maid all afternoon
trying to decide what's for supper.

> *You see how happy*
> *our natives are.*
> *Sundrum, seatree*
> *no need to scavenge.*

My Hawaii summer was hell.
Bobbed from doctor to doctor
more infections than a prostitute.

> *Always that bit slipping*
> *out of the frame.*

My man thinks I'm crazy.
First time I fainted
dropped right in his rucksack.
Clock wouldn't move. 10:27.

> *Why are you crying?*

I lied about the cards.
That was Joan Crawford
in *Rain*. Solitaire.

> *Last winter you fought*
> *to put words on the page.*

Lost. Took pictures.
Proved snow to myself
chemical tropics, the faucet.

> *This life is conducive.*
> *Not our fault.*

What's happened to the studio days?
Sprinklers pocking fake sand,
rubber palms, Madras hanging…

> *"Long before the stars were torn down…"*

Just look at the bathroom
cats lapping blood clumps
I'm afraid it's my mother's
off cloudy suds.

> *Please darken the bubbles with ink.*
> *Fill in the best advice*
> *you've ever gotten.*

Came to me slimy, color of jade.
"Let nothingness into your shots."

Working Girl, Perpignan

Dijon mostaza drips off a weenie
        Ste Marie Plage

Jezebel's craving an angular haircut
        uncherished blonde. Trashy girlhood

she changed locks like *Marnie*
screamed her way up from the trailer.

Her royal blue bikini's

        a universe center clasped bronze
that sags on the wasting Christ's thighs.

        Careful! His blood's only ketchup.

J & J Radio: Island Girl Dialogue

"I think it's a matter of being flighty
landing in both my lives…"

Joan Crawford wore a 4C shoe
Betty Boop statuettes
white-patent in *Rain*
still grand at the end-dawn

      muck-stained black patches
      on the heels of her fishnets.

If I'd been born scrappy
broomstick-bruised back
             indelible brows

arched sunrise, sunset
           you'd never know it.

~

Sadie descends on tamales in Madras.
Reformers talk her over
like she isn't home.

           She's right, though, huh?
       The worst is the brightness.

~

I'm here to buy a license
to name a cat Pele

the Joan waiting roadside
headscarfed
           hitching a ride
back to her crater.

I've hung on doorframes
looked ill without makeup
prayed evenings away.

> *You ever lost*
> *a library card?*

I've lived in a tent
listening to phonographs

kissed the blonde cherub face
day of my wedding in a lotus bog
      aisles and aisles of waste.

Think Lane Everett, the carnival
girl in her 40s, Joan reborn softer
not yet berserk.
Political bride
      house on Olympus
      the exotic life culminates
      in *Flamingo Road*.

Got away from it all
by the sin of my teeth
      damp hands puddling a .22
      under your mink.

Thirty days in the clink
and I'm back at my temple
shriney and new.

Working Girl 2

The Riviera's more subtle? Pastels?

         Cooler than it has been. Not bad. Jezebel
contemplates impossible launch

off the slab of lapis lazuli
the catching herself

before her top half goes under.
Salt does not mix with the stereotypical

Lux-soapéd blonde. The Toulousian jewelress
wrapped the junk like a treasure

helped the man match his wife to a watch
topped with a ribbon

        cleavage dripping black and white dots.
        Jezebel pretends her mom was Joan Crawford

as Sadie Thompson, that they owned a rouge broom.
She's not afraid of plastic bag sex

an Air France-striped bikini or grease
all trussed up like a prop, Perpignan.

Island Girl 2

As the single candle and the flames off the hotplate
glint certainly on the rainbars of cage...

Sadie'd shove a pogo stick
  up her cunt if you'd pay her
likes the sound of *lives*

but the wives slam the door in her face
  so quickly you'd think she had smallpox

Prison will evaporate at sunrise
  sand in her eye   Max Factor tear
creasing her cheek

No telephones on Pago Pago
  in her wake the equator

*

Sadie 2 is perlaceous, make-up-less, prostrate

slides the penitent in penitentiary

Joe Horn reads Ecclesiastes through the dark beats of witch
   but missing this part is not a slit throat

Walter Houston convulses
  slips off Sadie the Second's white nightie

*

So prison evaporates

  Sadie fastens her belt through its last handsome notch
swings the fox stole back over her shoulders

Belle-Soeur

The painted Mary sleeps beside the water demi-summers
foie-grasing fuzzy ducklings
in her heart-shaped gypsy trailer.

The Great Colonis burn the trunks of money
should have kept the crepe suzette.

Of course we feminize the river
curve her like the torso
of Gina Lollabrigida
call her brief soubrette

Our Lady Redlight Special
in the sunrise sense.

Holiday, Cuba
(Theo and Norma)

NORMA [to herself, playing *Reverie* on the piano]:
Sky's clouding up.
Sustain, sustain.

THEO [jolly, out loud]: Hold that note.

N: *Ruby-throated sunrise,*
could you be my time?
I'm so tired every thing is a symbol.

T: Very sorry for Avis, though I'm not sure what happened.

*

N: *Cancer means lobster.*
Pisces means bite.
Red spots on my legs.

[out loud]: You know I'm so haunted
by the sphinx in that book.
Reminds me of a Tanning
I saw in the Tate.
Next time I came they'd put it away.

T: London's no good for you.
That jack with the brushcut
follows you over bridges.

N: When it's blindingly sunny, it's safe!
And the shawl Avis wore
how it faded—

T: Let's buy a houseboat
in your precious Florida.

N: My first time in Miami
room numbers were written
above doorways in French.

I bought a bottle
of orange blossom cologne
trapped flower inside it
instead of a shark.

[to herself]: *Cinq, cinq, cinq.*

T: Why don't you practice
ring your eyes in make-up
let no sleep have its say?

N: You make women sick!
First Blanche, now me.

*

T: You've read Beckett, yes?
He writes of sand.

N: Of course. *Happy Days*
reminds me of Blanche.

T: My wife never reads.
Gator for breakfast or mango?

N [blowing powder in his face]:
Grapefruit and a ride on the beach.

T: In your negligée? May I join you?

*

N [riding alone, still thinking of Avis]:
How did she let it happen?
How *did* she?

Does art slide back to sea noiselessly?

My mind disintegrates
unweaves as we canter.
It's over, I Appaloosen...

[The pony throws Norma who cracks like a coconut shell.]

*

DOCTOR: I'm afraid it's a case
of poetic laryngitis.

Check her maidenform daily,
keep her out of swamps.

N [scratchily, making fists]:
I'll die in the Everglades
before I learn to sign *I love you.*

T: Darling, you'll make a beautiful mime!

Flaming June
(Blanche and Charlie)

Watercress?

    Yes. Pass the mayonnaise.

Charlie, I stroke my uterus orange.
Thirteen of you garden
kaleidoscopic outside

my beveled glass window.
This is a metaphor.
You are a snapdragon.

    Yes, marigold.

You never told me you wrote.

    I don't write
    I make songs
    while I ride the tractor.

Sing some. I'll hum.

    My love is a sprinkler hose
    my love is a peasant-boy pose
    frying eggs for my love

    and her husband's in Boise
    let's hope he blows
    his nose off in Ketchum…

Enough, prickly pear! I've got a tale.

Crunching shaved ice
in Aix-on-Provence
Theo pushing me
in my wicker wheelchair

I watched a redhead
dancing flamenco.

    I'm.Your.Teddybear.
    [Gyrates like Elvis.]

I'm wearing a half-slip
the colors of sunset
tiered like her dress.
Take off your clothes.

    Not yet, petunia.

Who are you kidding?
Your dick is a cucumber.
The locusts are clacking

like castanets.

    Let's move to Reno
    my Venus flytrap.

Sure. We'll eat sand
with platinum flatware.
Newsflash, we need cash, babe. *His* cash.

    [In Paul McCartney's "low" voice]
    You never give me your money
    you only give me your funny—

I'm dying in ivory under the lattice.
Pastels don't flatter my skintone.

*Sitting in an English garden
waiting for the sun...*

God, to mouthwash my brain,
rinse the last thirty years!

*...and if the sun don't come
you'll get a tan
from standin' in the English rain...*

Charlie! My medicine, please.
But first, taste this tea.

[Unbeknownst to Charlie
Blanche has sweetened
the poppyseed brew

with lotus blossoms.
Once he collapses,
she drops asleep in the heat.]

Sorry, Wrong Number
(Blanche)

Hello, hello?
Can you help me please?

I'm a cardiac neurotic.
My trouble's erotic.

My daughter's in the Poconos
drinking Merlot.

An admirer of Hemingway
my husband's in Idaho.

I've no one to tell.

*

A bride, I was fire

afraid my nipples
would burn smoke holes

through my bodice's
old-world embroidery,

zirconium strings
ringing my knees,

my life *Lucia di Lammermoor*.

*

Plan of attack? No plan.

No attack. The honeymoon
rose, set all that.

Legs closed, I took to my bed
faking seizures. The doctor said I couldn't

sustain making love, *please don't
touch her.*

*

Every morning Charlie
crumbles my morphine
in orange juice

kneads my right shoulder
to pulp. The first time
he kissed my forehead

I turned my lips away.
Next day he sat me on top of him

porcelain doll on a stick
hula-girl Venus

rolling my hips.
He reads the mail

from my husband,
fish are biting and horses

do love a brook
sniffs the musk in my armpits

bites my breasts violet
sets me on the floor on all fours

bears down on me hissing
I hope your knees bleed bitch.

Jezebel Interludes

    Jezebel tries to decide what sword she's avoiding
tokes on the right side of the Garonne
              lone vixen who'd fancy spurting a Rome, still writes
her teachers on die-cut butterflies
       begs every Toulousian to give a fuck about plagues.
                     Don your *pest medicin*, meditate on the sunny
          Perpignan sons, who'd rather eat rats than be French.

Jezebel 5(6)

Time lies suspended young pin-up

somewhere in France

a Grey Poupon-colored purse

waits, eighteen Euros

a man with a cart
sells fruit slushes, no sugar

    café au lait?

Well, Nescafé

*

On the way to Nogales
you ask about process
   my rat-chested cobbling

Thinking of Bishop's
    wooden clogs
carelessly clacking

I feed you fibs as we switch
to kilometers

    out here in the desert
    we call it maize

*

You're more interested in Europe than I
ecstatic that *Gigi*'s revived

I've let my façade oxidate—
but thank heaven
      for little girls—

(Remember, Jez, it's cliché
to write about bodies
might as well say
he spanked your thighs raw...)

    So what if he did?
    It was diabolique!

Not big on dawn sex?

Well, we never were twins
    not even mechanical cousins

different as light and day

Love in a Fireproof Box
(or Jezebel speaks to her Eva Phillips self)

                        Well, that tender breast was impeccable.
Two minutes too late.
              ♪: "I think I'll go for a walk outside. The summertime's
                calling my name, can you hear it now?"

Canter in your jodhpurs, but don't get too ambitious.
I'll practice collapsing my face in the mirror
smear my effects in cold crème.
                    Carole's legs dangled from the loft in the stable.
Couldn't put anything past her.
I liked her hair platinum until it got trashy.
Little chit rationed my sleeping pills. Nuts in her blood.

When I dyed my hair red, our bed smelt of mud.
Wonderful, dead old times!
                    Carole used her own socks for a noose
                    maniacally, edgewise.

[Phone rings.] Yes, sir. No sir. I miss your glow, sir. [Replaces the phone.]
So sneaky she should have clanged!

                    Don't you know how hard we have it
                    culling our thoughts into poems?

[Softly] Knowing when to let in?

Collect all her fingernail clippings!
Clone all her notes!

Jezebel, Out of the Nursery

She's not tired of poetry, she's tired of dark
  watching raccoons stuff her jack-the-ripper muck
in their mouths. Overusing "throat." She's had
  her meditative moments, waiting for rain
unable to pollute her soul with food
  processing a beverage of lemons and poinsettia.
(Blender looked like a vase until she turned it on.)

She's tired of pornography, breastmilk, and gingersnap
  always the culprit left clothed. She knows it's only
a plastic moon of a daytrip at HoJo. She'll sun
  and she'll read, write a short poem in leaves
round the Mexican flower, everything but the words
  she most needs to say.
      Jezebel dreams the sea is on fire!
      Someone's rolling
      gasoline balls down the falls!

It's acceptable to be a bit afraid of power
  meet once a week to regroup. Form is home
poemparts glittering inner tubes tan girls collect
  smoothly as hats. "Don't you like dance?"
the rich lady asks, slips toward the pool
  lyric lyre scared to touch the water
like it's crown jewels or a pre-mature baby. Jezebel laughs
  poems always end this way, poinsettias undead
but near dying, vanity sizes no one will bless.
      "Yes, I'm an extremist."
      "Why didn't you say so?"

4.

Preamble

Making a good shoe's just as hard as building an empire.

Explains how Lily Powers
worked her legs up that bank
chilly blonde in pointy collars
days the swanky music lied.

*
Please give me seconds to be tender, Lonely Lola Lo

smell coconuts, smooch moonlight, climb stems of boys in khaki.
I wanted to be magic
back arching like a cat

cleaving toes and popped corns
off the sobbing cobs.

This is why stiletto burn is worth it.

*
Gentlemen at ease!
Read Abelard and Eloise
pearlescent guides
to long-time loving.

I've learned I don't resent you.

I resent myself
only flesh and water
oxygen, some bone,
shrieking ukulele,
teary Deborah Kerr…

This is where the cash valise comes in.

                Navy-blue lips whisper
                life is pain but
                Lola shuts them.

"Mares eat oats and does eat oats"
Charles and Mary Lamb eat Shakespeare…

The sun is coming up   like a glittering geranium
    the way a Lady changes   when a groom walks in the room

The snow is contemplative, avocadoes throbbing
    as Jezebel seeds
       another Victory garden   children ducking under schoolbells

eating summer squash   binging on Bing Crosby

      except for Jean Jacques' offspring
                      who dine on arbitration

*

I predict this wedding is Cassandran
twist my hair like Tippi Hedren's
sign the card in felt-tipped ink

        I have had compulsions
              handwriting laborious
        I have had a god
              topped with hokey pokey
        I have had impatiens
        and the country mansion

Don't spend a shred of shame in missing.
Jezebel is solemn. And will merry again.

Mock Ghazaling in the Nursery

Night, paint, no new words in days. Automatic,
autocratic, ox, orthodox. Villette, Violette. Lucy Elucidate…

Governess Mary says my marginalia is art that gestates
in red fringes of history. So heavy I sneeze. You clarinet

so loudly I'm dumb, strapping, no, slapping
my bonnet-sense on, my fingers skinny calves

of a llama, my neurons neurotic. My fingers *not* necks
of swans, your suggestion benign, too Lady of the Lakey.

You're always the hoarder, semi-sweet, brainy brunette
antipest. Mary squeezes purple jelly in my mouth from her breasts

illuminates her sketchbooks with green light and paint.
Is Daddy home from Bucharest yet? I can't see the streetcar

through the stained glass you've lacquered, cornflower
to navy. He promised canaries, Rossettis, and rest. I'll strip off

my costume, unbraid my zest, prance on your temples.
Haven't had a new tunic since Mummycups died.

Mary says to be Dickinson, I must be myself
anxiety of influence a sugar-dough axis around which

my teapot should spin. Indeed, it's treat force, my vomit
blending in with the half-moons on your Persian carpet.

You know how to edit, asexual in the tunicate sense
cementing my poems in your conch, Jezebel.

When and If Jezebel Waxes Brunette

My blonde wanes, I'm not yet at the age
  my life can be seamless
Spring's mellowed, big-mouthed.

Please congratulate me
  on my scholarship to dolldom
a poem not at home in two columns.

I'm Jessica, hair one-oh-one. I've got brains
  invalided, I chop my sick mother
two Clauds ununited

until they meet Pilate and crash
  one blonde and swiss-dotted, one
brunette tropicalia who shakes her bouquet

splatters gold grease on the nursery walls.
  To continue these scenes, I need ambience
illuminación. Clarinda makes light

of my processes, gossiping through
  her pellucid telephone. *Unregarded couplets*
seeped into my dreams, then thunderclaps

snapped me in half. I smelled smoke.
  This poem would have satisfied once.
Now I hate raw material

cannot roll burgers in balls. Heidi-ho
  helping Clara hobble uphill
in her green smock on crutches

but I am Frau Nothing, Frau Frowsy
   Frau Ink. Jezebel is Laura Petrie
to my Sally or Pickles. Perhaps we should sleep

in twin beds? She's liable to leave, but I can't
   I'm too tempted by oxblood, the nursery chapel
Jez's brown flip, silhouetted stained glass.

Lucy Snowe Thinks *Dark Victory*, Cannot Commit Herself

Clunky phrases on a desk
  that doesn't feel like mine. Can't
think of her name. Cloud-cover somewhere
  flushed baby wresting himself
from his straps. *Judith Trahern*.
  Sandpaper your legs, ashen tulips
effective. Judith who can't light
  a match. Geraldine Fitzgerald
as Sweet Ann Assistant then the bitch
  who wouldn't give
the Corncracker ticket. The public loves shimmer
  parties and glittery hats. Sometimes we forget
the complexity of systems, how we fill time
  but each one won part of the winnings!
the way a brain runs. The one time I tried
  to be flighty and sun, a boy threw
a water-filled prophylactic at my ankle.

Jezebel Has the Same Mole as Alexis. Hers Is Not Velvet.

    Bleaching hair at home leads to nights
      without highlights, life spluttering
    resting on eyeballs. I'm not threatened by ice
      what they used to call beauty marks.

    Sweet pirate, retrace your steps. Say what
      you want me to say.
                      I can't leave yet
I have not my skull, lack the skill to transform
from peasant to courtesan, daubing on cordblood.

    I swallowed the lid
    to my liquor bottle, told all
    I'd swallowed the lock, hap, hap
    happy to snap brittle time.

Why Jezebel Writes Saturday
(She Could Be Sleeping)

The need for a sea shanty
  venerating the Venus
who washed up on the glacier

while she was out sailing
  with Gina Lollabrigida
and Bette Davis, allaying the pleasure

she takes in fishing, a seal town
  bronchitis, eyewipes to swab
Persian cat faces. Brachycephalic

the need for a gimmick.
  "This fog is so thick
condensation made sausage,"

Bette says, clipped, though
  it would sound more authentic
if Gina had said it. Jeepers
  creepers, the need for a sea…

Jezebel Intermezzos

Windy out there. Mary makes the monster.
Mae West creates Mae West. W.C. Fields
raises a strikingly high I.Q.
for someone who habitually drinks embalming fluid.
Jezebel does not lack intensity
a city near Budapest
knows she's left of aim when she shoots.
"Better than commas," says Flower Belle Lee
exploding the smoldering porcelain mallards.

Poseidon Adventure, Plus One

> *"I'm finally ready for* The Long Night
> *prelude to a kill. Annie Dvorak, Vinnie Price*
> *sadistic magician. Gas mask, flower shoppe*
> *not unlike my own. You could put my*
> *two and two together..."*

No surprise in this writer
all night in the filling station
ordering chili dogs
ten-dollar mesh sandals with sage.

Descending the stairs in my Dutch negligée
pretending I had sweet sleep
I unwrap a new sketchbook. Jezebel shrieks.

Lachrymary Shelley's in the parlor
clucking up the pasteboard stage
cloth-diapering the manger
for her baby neverwas.

I waltz through the kitchen, plunging drains
pestling dead pretzels to paprika.

> A little sad, a little blue
> a little cervicitis
> but breasts sublime at seventeen
> and what albedo!

There's got to be a pre-lapsarian elegance to eggs...

> Mary named the baby Clara
> for the mother of Allegra
> Claire (née Jane) Clairmont

        who'd changed her name to be poetic
        after looking at her face
        dog-paddling on the surface of the lake.
        (Mark Twain called the lion of Lucerne
        the saddest piece of rock on earth.)

There's got to be a poignancy to these angeled eggs
or maybe I'm just jealous, mourning after...

Poseidon Adventure, Plus Two

I wake feeling so sane it's making me sick
strut into the bedroom, miming "Dejection: An Ode"
coddling too much my words, Jezebel says,
swaddling each wretched oval in the gauze of the Oxford.

Mary's swabbing merthiolade on the neck of the faucet
won't let me drink enough coffee, says she can
brighten my nightmares to neon-maned ponies
who'll swirl their legs peacefully in the Garonne.

I keep my legs crossed to uphold my bladder
I've not popped out children, my future's still solid.
Mary's is cracked, beet bleat stains on her bodice,
looks like she's lactating terracotta. She has room to talk

what's her mistresspiece if not a yellow-eyed, thin-lipped
black dream? I've broken a cherry in my hot tea
to sweeten my read. Deep France was so French
I can't translate. The rose city smelled like

a chapel of rest, bright on its surface, no undertone.
Does a conscientious gothic framing take pressure off?
I keep my belly big, rounding out poems, need
that balance of context. Jezebel's fluent in French

says writing ironically's nothing short of a crime.
Possibilities are limited, we're spinning in time
sharpening our spinnerets, watching our fingers.
My pale nails scream anemia, illegitimate kidneys,

Mary's left pinky indicates unforgiving.
We played Ancient Mariner the whole way from Calais.

For Mary, Miscarriage

Sacrilegious epiphany.   Pretty squash.
    "Expecting" a temporary state

fetus Charles Laughton   treat him as such
    milquetoast who will not drink skim

unless you're Elsa Lanchester   acting Louise Patterson

punchy hormones and *The Big Clock*   never stops ticking

perpetually pregnant or painting…what difference?

But a visit from Daddycups   sets you on track.   You root
    through the Wonderland dumpster   eat ovary pie

adore more and more
the chamois of lies

Percy calls "romantic creation."   These days, invitro's

clear as the sky.

Poseidon Adventure, Plus Three

It makes a difference when you educate abroad.
Mary goes to Ladywitch's nursing school
with Jezebel. I stay home, penning poems
in the ecru parlor, rib bones
dipped in ink. Martha is marigenous
hammering the song of shipwreck
on her sealskin xylophone.

Terms of marriageability? Dry hunger's one.
The willingness to pray to rats
who gnaw on marigolds another.
The hydrolysis of lactose
into glucose and galactose,
a fingernail that whips
our silky ways into the air.

When Shelley marries Mary
we'll chant a palindrome
know Candlemas is over,
Mary lilies as maturative
as the pussey lung infection
I caught lapping up the Big Splash
watching Shelley Winters
balance on the fulcrum

of John Garfield's arm
before he took her home
and held her family hostage.
The physicality of passage
haunts my contemplative nature.
Soaking dishes makes me dangerous.
I hold the filthy candle
seven different ways to save it
as if I had the choice to leave Poseidon.

Theme Song (a straight, light, and peppy poem)

The shop by the seashore sells wicked seating
Belladonna Reed skips her non-existent nap
      buys the wrong chaise lounge   brownbags it with champagne
        spills her shells and wedding rings   across the sawdust floor

Belles letters are too heavy   one more family calamity
        lungs and pores

Myra the psychic says the baby isn't hers
It's bugging her through dinner
She won't let the whetting doll alone

                        Mae West had an hourglass figure?
                        Yes. Three-hundred-sixty degrees

Is Belladonna your warming-pan?
Is Belladonna your albatross?
Please tell her not to worry
                        even clairvoyants will get foggy

Are those the sands of time
squeaking through her cervix
or the kittiwakes a-screaming?

Letter to Mary from Jezebel

I've got a system, part weedy chin hairs
   part obligato. I'll live on this boat
like it's a resort, write to buoy up
   the dry stretch. I'm stick-to-your-pistols
productive. First mate shoves a gun
   in my back. He won't come to the wedding
though he made a great show
   of logging your date. Absence of sun
bone-in pity, teen pregnancy rates
   high on calm seas, can't hide in the cabin
can't read through the storm. I'll lie
   on the deck, languish in custody
of maritime laws, not yet to the state
   where I drink my own piss.
First mate's gondolierish in stripes
   sounding my uterus by the point
of his oar. Mornings, I still dream
   of London, tiger lilies encoffined
on St. Paul's Cathedral.

Poseidon Adventure, Plus Four

Our ship sails belauded
to the leper island.
Sing a song of nymphos
speckling the sky.

Martha's longing for the inner life
Mary claims is overrated.
Creativity is labor.
She paces, checks the clock.

When the candle's melting low
its wick floats like her cervix.
I want to walk beside the sea
   sing a song of nymphos
   (speckling the sky)
but Jezebel's waxed futile
streaked her hair brunette.

How many lines have I lost
over ivory geraniums?
Teresa Delgado lost her life
about a bag of flour

spectrumed from hysterical
to not afraid at all.
My biggest fear is filling
horizontal time. The cat

is a barometer, his long tail
merits language.
Should I hoard my eggs
or share them with the colony?
Might I contract leprosy
rubbing Margeaux's castanets?

Another Morning After

Call it counterintuitive
    Kate Greenaway splitting a thin cigarette
    with Sydney Greenstreet
    Pete Lorre scratching sweepstakes tickets
    behind the ice machine

but there's something French in deprivation
something crippled about sex.

A polioed uncle presses powder
on the Prussian face of Madeleine
the bellicose murderess in her antebellum dress.
Since you wrote this, it will happen

but Jezebel must finish
your Jack-the-Ripper poem
if she is, indeed, our authoress.

Belladonna's fucking like a virgin
burning through her innards, tuppance at the wharf.
    You thought you saw her
     pussycat? You thought you saw my island?
    You thought you saw the nightmares
    I shove down my throat?

    Vultures ply my ulcers
    cold callers rock the boat
    switch back, and I'll be happy.

Notes

The poems listed below engage with the works of art listed with them. (Unless otherwise noted, the italicized titles are those of films.)

Section 1

"The Appledoppeling Gang": *A Stolen Life*
"Jezebel, Jealous of Television": *Whatever Happened to Baby Jane?*
"This Is the 20th Century, and We Get to New York on Time": *20th Century*, this poem is narrated by the character Lily Garland (Carole Lombard)
"Restless Palms": The title is a phrase from the Bob Dylan song "Spanish Harlem Incident."
"Tale of Three Cities": *Dark Passage*
"Vivisect the Creamy Sister": *The Dragon Painter*
"Jezebel Keeps the Appointment": *Midnight Express, Diabolique*

Section 2

The Lucies are derivatives of the character Lucy Snowe from Charlotte Brontë's novel *Villette*.
"Lucy in Wien, Looking at Brueghel's *Hunters in Snow*" joins a (primarily male) coterie of poems about Brueghel's paintings such as those written by Williams, Auden, and Ashberry.
"Lucy to Erzebet, Watching *Conquest*": *Conquest, The Petrified Forest*
"Eagle, Moose, Grizzly   Revisited": *Three Strangers*
"Merrily": *Today We Live*
"Thrift": *Remember the Night*

Section 3

"Island Girl," "Working Girl, Perpignan," "J & J Radio: Island Girl Dialogue," "Working Girl 2," and "Island Girl 2" depend heavily upon *Rain* and less heavily upon *Flamingo Road*. "Long before the stars were torn down" is a line from "Brownsville Girl" by Bob Dylan. "Let nothingness into your shots" is from a "Golf Zen" calendar.

"Holiday, Cuba": Avis is the title character in *The Story of Avis*, a novel by Elizabeth Stuart Phelps.

"Flaming June" was motivated, in part, by the painting of the same name by Lord Frederic Leighton.

"Love in a Fireproof Box": *Queen Bee*

Section 4

"Preamble": *Baby Face, From Here to Eternity*
"Lucy Snowe Thinks *Dark Victory*, Cannot Commit Herself": *Dark Victory, Three Strangers*
"Jezebel Intermezzos": *My Little Chickadee*
"For Mary, Miscarriage": *The Big Clock*
"Poseidon Adventure, Plus Three": *He Ran All the Way*
"Poseidon Adventure, Plus Four": *The Leopard Man*

The last eight poems of this section take, as their implied refrain, the lyric "There's got to be a morning after..." from the theme song of the film *The Poseidon Adventure*. These poems also draw upon the life and work of Mary Shelley, both real and imagined.

Jessie Janeshek grew up in West Virginia and earned a B.A. from Bethany College, an M.F.A. from Emerson College, and a Ph.D. from the University of Tennessee–Knoxville. Her first book is *Outscape: Writings on Fences and Frontiers*, a literary anthology she co-edited in 2008. She teaches writing at the University of Tennessee, works as a freelance editor, and promotes her belief in the power of creative writing as community outreach by co-directing a variety of volunteer poetry workshops. She lives in Knoxville with her man and three cats.